ANIMALS
in Camouflage

Phyllis Limbacher Tildes

ini Charlesbridge

I blend with the snow as I roam the ice floes of the Arctic in search of fat seals.

I have a big, furry body and large, powerful paws.

What am I?

a polar bear

I can eat one hundred
pounds in one meal.
When my cubs are old
enough to leave the den,
I teach them to hunt.

My large, leathery wings look like the bright green leaves that I love to eat. I can even tremble like a leaf in the breeze.

What am I?

a leaf insect

I am also called the walking leaf. Like my cousin the walking stick, I am disguised as a plant to hide from birds, snakes, and other predators.

I rest by day, hidden high in the shady branches of a tree.

At night I take flight. With my wings spread wide, I silently swoop to scoop up my prey.

What am I?

a great horned owl

I am also known as the hoot owl. My call is an echoing, *"Hoo, hoo-hoo-hoo, hoo-oo, hoo-oo."*

I am a fierce hunter,
catching rabbits, mice,
and snakes to feed
my hungry owlets.

I wait on the petals of a flower, ready to pounce on beetles, bees, and flies.

My body is shaped like a crab, and I can walk sideways and backward.

What am I?

a crab spider

Unlike most spiders,
I do not spin a web.
I can slowly change my
color to match the yellow
or white flowers on
which I can be found.

I look like a
little dragon
hiding in gently
waving seaweed.

My long snout is
like a vacuum hose
sucking in tiny
creatures.

What am I?

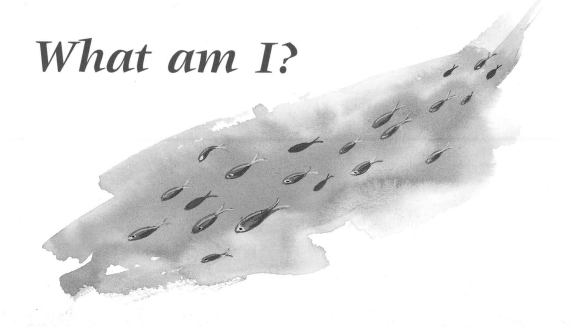

a leafy sea dragon

I am a fish related to the sea horse. I live in the coastal waters of southern Australia. My leafy "arms" often fool big, hungry fish.

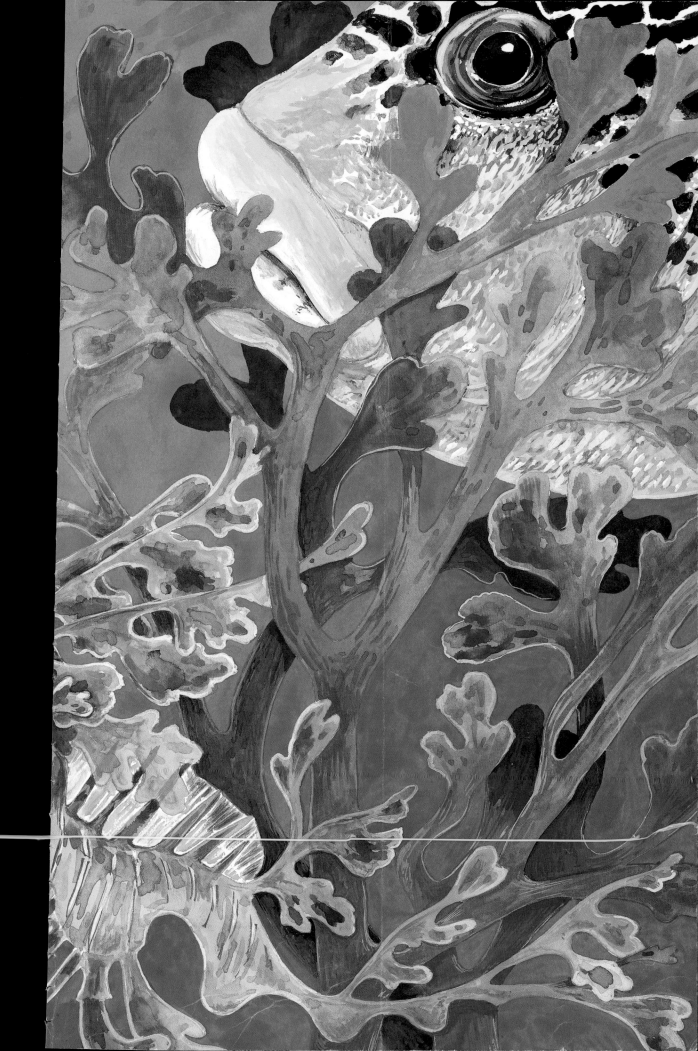

I hide in a thicket, blending with the sunlight and shadows on the forest floor.

I have camouflage spots that will disappear when I am older.

What am I?

a fawn

I am a baby white-tailed deer. My mother is called a doe. My father is a buck and has large antlers for fighting other male deer.

It is easy being green because I blend with the leaves around me. I can even change to yellow or brown.

From high in a moonlit tree or across a sparkling pond, I sing my spring song.

What am I?

a tree frog

I have round suction cups
at the ends of my fingers
and toes to help me climb.

To attract a female mate,
I puff out the sac under
my chin and croak
for hours.

Did you know?

Animals use camouflage to hide from both predators and unsuspecting prey. Some of the most successful methods of camouflage are BLENDING (the animal's natural color matches or blends with its surroundings), COLOR CHANGE (the animal's color changes to match its background), DISGUISE (the animal looks like another animal or object), and PATTERN (the animal's spots or stripes break up its shape).

BLENDING

The **polar bear** is the largest predator on land. The male can weigh up to fifteen hundred pounds and be as tall as twelve feet when standing on his hind legs. Usually the female gives birth to two cubs, which she nurses and protects for two years. The polar bear swims gracefully in icy water, insulated with two layers of fur and a thick layer of blubber. With large, partially webbed paws, it can swim for up to sixty miles without resting.

DISGUISE

The shape, color, and trembling movement of the **Ceylon leaf insect** create the illusion of a green leaf. The female's large wings are patterned like the veins of a leaf. Her eggs look like seeds, and the newly hatched young are reddish, just like the buds on some branches. The babies turn green soon after they begin to eat leaves. The leaf insect is found in India, Australia, Southeast Asia, and the South Pacific. There are about twenty-five species in all.

BLENDING

The **great horned owl** is the heaviest and most powerful owl in North and South America. It has a wingspan of three to four and one-half feet. With its excellent night vision, sharp hearing, and large talons, it can easily capture small mammals. It can even attack prey as large as a skunk or fox. Although the tufts on the great horned owl's head look like ears or horns, they are actually feathers that help the owl to blend with the bark and branches of a tree.

COLOR CHANGE

There are many **crab spider** species around the world. This crab spider is *Misumena vatia*, also called the white death spider. It attacks the insects that wander onto the white or yellow flowers where it hunts, paralyzes them, and sucks out their juices. It can take up to ten days for the crab spider to change its color. The female is much larger than the male. She will kill the male after mating unless he is quick and clever.

DISGUISE

The **leafy sea dragon** is a marine fish that grows to about seventeen inches in length. It has tiny fins on its head and back that propel it through the seaweed "jungles" in which it hides. It breeds in shallow water in early summer. The female deposits up to three hundred eggs on the male's tail in an area called a brood patch. The male carries the eggs until they hatch.

PATTERN

The **white-tailed deer** gives birth to up to three spotted fawns in late spring in the forests of North America. A wobbly, newborn fawn can stand within thirty minutes of birth. Hidden in tall grass or under shady leaves, the baby lies very still while its mother grazes nearby. The doe nurses the fawn until it is strong enough to graze with her. By fall the fawn's spots have begun to fade. The following spring the yearling will leave its mother when she gives birth again.

COLOR CHANGE

The **European tree frog** is about two inches long. Only the male tree frog sings and has an expandable vocal sac. After mating, the female lays a cluster of eggs in a pond. Larvae hatch and slowly become tadpoles. In about two and one-half months the tadpoles become air-breathing amphibians with four feet. If they avoid being captured by birds, snakes, or other predators, the young frogs will thrive, eating insects such as ants and mosquitoes.

for Sol Mitchell,
with love

with special thanks to my editor, Yolanda LeRoy
— P. L. T.

Published by Charlesbridge Publishing
85 Main Street, Watertown, MA 02472
(617) 926-0329
www.charlesbridge.com

Library of Congress Cataloging-in-Publication Data
Tildes, Phyllis Limbacher.
Animals in camouflage/Phyllis Limbacher Tildes.
p.   cm.
Summary: Describes how various animals use their coloration and physical
characteristics to conceal themselves.
ISBN 0-88106-120-4 (reinforced for library use)
ISBN 0-88106-134-4 (softcover)
1. Camouflage (Biology)—Juvenile literature.
[1. Camouflage (Biology) 2. Animals.] I. Title.
QL759.T55 2000
591.47'2—dc21   99-18762

Printed in the United States of America
(hc) 10 9 8 7 6 5 4 3 2 1
(sc) 10 9 8 7 6 5 4 3 2 1

The illustrations in this book were done in gouache on
Strathmore 4-ply illustration paper, kid finish.
The display type and text type were set in
Impact and Veljovik by Diane M. Earley.
Color separations were made by Eastern Rainbow, Derry, New Hampshire.
Printed and bound by Worzalla Publishing Company, Stevens Point, Wisconsin
Production supervision by Brian G. Walker
Designed by Phyllis Limbacher Tildes
This book was printed on recycled paper.